The first period can b ~~[barcode: CW01370734]~~ ..., but when you approach it consciously, you can be sure that nothing will surprise you and that the fear will pass quickly. See what you should know about the first period and how to prepare for it.

Puberty is a time of many changes. At the end of this period, girls experience their first periods. This is an important stage of development. It means that you are becoming biologically adult and that your body is getting ready to have children in the future.

The first period, technically known as the menarche, usually occurs between the ages of 11 and 14. However, these are not rigid standards. The first menstruation at age 10 is nothing to worry about or worry about. It is worth telling about it at the next visit to the attending pediatrician. Even if you're 14 and still don't have periods, you don't have to worry that something is wrong. When the first period occurs depends on many individual circumstances. Genetic factors play an important role. You can ask your mom what age was her first period. But don't be overwhelmed by it, because these days environmental factors and diet also have an influence. Overall health, exercise, and weight also play a role. As you can see, it is not that simple and you cannot speed it up or slow it down.

Each girl matures differently and the period can come at different ages. There is no point in comparing yourself with your friends and worrying in advance. Remember that most little women mature properly, only at their own pace. Reasons for concern include having the first period before the age of 10, or not having it after the age of 16. Then consultation with a doctor may be necessary.

Symptoms of the first menstruation

You've probably noticed that your body has been changing for a long time. The silhouette took on a feminine shape: your hips became rounded, your breasts grew, pubic hair appeared, as well as on your legs and armpits. Your height has probably changed, and acne may have appeared. As you already know, the first menstruation occurs at the end of puberty. So you can expect it, although it usually occurs unexpectedly. Usually, before this big day, there are no bothersome ailments. However, each organism is different and the symptoms are individual.

The most common and characteristic signs of the first period include:

-spotting or light bleeding for several days,
-the appearance of white discharge,
-pain and cramps in the lower abdomen,
-slight weakness and general malaise,
-nausea,
-irritability, distraction, and mood swings.

The symptoms of the first period may vary and may vary in severity. It is worth observing changes in your body and being prepared.

In the case of what the first period looks like, there is no single answer either. If you discuss this topic with your friends, be prepared that everyone may say something different. The usual question is: how long is the first period? It can be different. It is worth noting that the first periods are irregular and may last from 3 to 7 days. Also, the appearance of another one is not obvious and it is normal for several months between periods. Your first period may be very light (a few drops of blood) or very heavy. The color of the discharge can also vary - both blood red and brown are the norm. As for soreness, the first bleeds are usually not painful. Then it can be different because many women suffer from this type of ailments. Fortunately, they pass with menstruation.

At this point, it is worth noting that the first six years after the appearance of the first period is the time to regulate the level of hormones. After this time, menstruation will be quite systematic and will take place on average in 28-day cycles. However, initially, you may have irregular periods. This has to do with the fact that the first cycles are often still anovulatory. Remember that this is not a rule and cannot be treated as a period in which pregnancy is impossible.

The first menstruation - how to prepare?

If you suspect that you may start menstruating soon, don't be afraid of it. It is natural for you to mature and period is a sign of proper development. If you feel anxious talk to someone you are in good contact with. It can be mom, older sister, grandmother, or aunt. It's normal to want to know what it all looks like and what to do then. Also, remember that girlfriends will not always have the appropriate knowledge. It is worth talking to someone who will listen to your concerns, as well as share their experiences and knowledge of the topic with you. If you still have any doubts, it is worth talking to e.g. a gynecologist who will explain exactly what is happening to your body. In addition, it will be a reliable source of information.

Don't be afraid to ask, it's normal to feel stressed in front of an unfamiliar situation. If you are aware and well prepared for what awaits you, you will stop worrying and calmly wait for your first period.

You can also prepare yourself on the practical side. Go shopping with someone you trust to learn about and choose the appropriate hygiene measures for your period. It is worth having, for example, a sanitary napkin in your backpack or purse. Proper hygiene during your period is also important. This is important in preventing infection. There are many products on the market for teenagers, including special intimate cleansers.

THE VERY PRACTICAL THING ABOUT EVERY ADOLESCENT GIRL IS THE PERIOD TRACKER.

CURRENTLY, THE PERIOD TRACKER IS PRIMARILY USED TO MONITOR YOUR MENSTRUAL CYCLE AND PREDICT WHEN THE NEXT PERIOD WILL APPEAR. SUCH RECORDS ARE ESPECIALLY USEFUL DURING A VISIT TO A GYNECOLOGIST - A DOCTOR, SEEING A RECORD OF MANY PREVIOUS PERIODS, CAN MORE EASILY DETECT POSSIBLE IRREGULARITIES IN THE LENGTH OF THE CYCLE OR OBSERVE WHY THE PERIOD OCCURS SO IRREGULARLY.

HOW TO USE THE PERIOD TRACKER?

JUST FILL IN THE DIARY DILIGENTLY AND YOU WILL NEVER BE SURPRISED BY THE PERIOD!

DATE:_____ PERIOD DAY #_____

FLOW: 🌢 LIGHT   🌢🌢 MEDIUM   🌢🌢🌢 HEAVY

I'M FEELING...

HAPPY   SAD   ANGRY   TIRED   ANNOYED   SCARED

ANY SYMPTOMS?

CRAMPS   SORE BREASTS   HEAD ACHE   BATHROOM TROUBLE   NAUSEA   ACNE

NOTES
_____
_____
_____

DATE:_____ PERIOD DAY #_____

FLOW: 🌢 LIGHT   🌢🌢 MEDIUM   🌢🌢🌢 HEAVY

I'M FEELING...

HAPPY   SAD   ANGRY   TIRED   ANNOYED   SCARED

ANY SYMPTOMS?

CRAMPS   SORE BREASTS   HEAD ACHE   BATHROOM TROUBLE   NAUSEA   ACNE

NOTES
_____
_____
_____

DATE:_____ PERIOD DAY # _____

FLOW: ◊ LIGHT   ◊◊ MEDIUM   ◊◊◊ HEAVY

I'M FEELING...

HAPPY   SAD   ANGRY   TIRED   ANNOYED   SCARED

ANY SYMPTOMS?

CRAMPS   SORE BREASTS   HEAD ACHE   BATHROOM TROUBLE   NAUSEA   ACNE

NOTES
_____
_____
_____

DATE:_____ PERIOD DAY # _____

FLOW: ◊ LIGHT   ◊◊ MEDIUM   ◊◊◊ HEAVY

I'M FEELING...

HAPPY   SAD   ANGRY   TIRED   ANNOYED   SCARED

ANY SYMPTOMS?

CRAMPS   SORE BREASTS   HEAD ACHE   BATHROOM TROUBLE   NAUSEA   ACNE

NOTES
_____
_____
_____

DATE:_____   PERIOD DAY #_____

FLOW: ◊ LIGHT   ◊◊ MEDIUM   ◊◊◊ HEAVY

I'M FEELING...

HAPPY   SAD   ANGRY   TIRED   ANNOYED   SCARED

ANY SYMPTOMS?

CRAMPS   SORE BREASTS   HEAD ACHE   BATHROOM TROUBLE   NAUSEA   ACNE

NOTES
_____
_____
_____

DATE:_____   PERIOD DAY #_____

FLOW: ◊ LIGHT   ◊◊ MEDIUM   ◊◊◊ HEAVY

I'M FEELING...

HAPPY   SAD   ANGRY   TIRED   ANNOYED   SCARED

ANY SYMPTOMS?

CRAMPS   SORE BREASTS   HEAD ACHE   BATHROOM TROUBLE   NAUSEA   ACNE

NOTES
_____
_____
_____

DATE:_____ PERIOD DAY #_____

FLOW: 🌢 LIGHT   🌢🌢 MEDIUM   🌢🌢🌢 HEAVY

I'M FEELING...

😊 HAPPY   😢 SAD   😠 ANGRY   😴 TIRED   😤 ANNOYED   😧 SCARED

ANY SYMPTOMS?

CRAMPS   SORE BREASTS   HEAD ACHE   BATHROOM TROUBLE   NAUSEA   ACNE

NOTES
_____
_____
_____

DATE:_____ PERIOD DAY #_____

FLOW: 🌢 LIGHT   🌢🌢 MEDIUM   🌢🌢🌢 HEAVY

I'M FEELING...

😊 HAPPY   😢 SAD   😠 ANGRY   😴 TIRED   😤 ANNOYED   😧 SCARED

ANY SYMPTOMS?

CRAMPS   SORE BREASTS   HEAD ACHE   BATHROOM TROUBLE   NAUSEA   ACNE

NOTES
_____
_____
_____

DATE:_____ PERIOD DAY #_____

FLOW: ○ LIGHT ○○ MEDIUM ○○○ HEAVY

I'M FEELING...

HAPPY   SAD   ANGRY   TIRED   ANNOYED   SCARED

ANY SYMPTOMS?

CRAMPS   SORE BREASTS   HEAD ACHE   BATHROOM TROUBLE   NAUSEA   ACNE

NOTES
_____
_____
_____

DATE:_____ PERIOD DAY #_____

FLOW: ○ LIGHT ○○ MEDIUM ○○○ HEAVY

I'M FEELING...

HAPPY   SAD   ANGRY   TIRED   ANNOYED   SCARED

ANY SYMPTOMS?

CRAMPS   SORE BREASTS   HEAD ACHE   BATHROOM TROUBLE   NAUSEA   ACNE

NOTES
_____
_____
_____

DATE:_____ PERIOD DAY #_____

FLOW: ◊ LIGHT ◊◊ MEDIUM ◊◊◊ HEAVY

I'M FEELING...

HAPPY SAD ANGRY TIRED ANNOYED SCARED

ANY SYMPTOMS?

CRAMPS SORE BREASTS HEAD ACHE BATHROOM TROUBLE NAUSEA ACNE

NOTES _____
_____
_____

DATE:_____ PERIOD DAY #_____

FLOW: ◊ LIGHT ◊◊ MEDIUM ◊◊◊ HEAVY

I'M FEELING...

HAPPY SAD ANGRY TIRED ANNOYED SCARED

ANY SYMPTOMS?

CRAMPS SORE BREASTS HEAD ACHE BATHROOM TROUBLE NAUSEA ACNE

NOTES _____
_____
_____

DATE:_____ PERIOD DAY #_____

FLOW: ◌ LIGHT ◌◌ MEDIUM ◌◌◌ HEAVY

I'M FEELING...

HAPPY SAD ANGRY TIRED ANNOYED SCARED

ANY SYMPTOMS?

CRAMPS SORE BREASTS HEAD ACHE BATHROOM TROUBLE NAUSEA ACNE

NOTES
_____
_____
_____

DATE:_____ PERIOD DAY #_____

FLOW: ◌ LIGHT ◌◌ MEDIUM ◌◌◌ HEAVY

I'M FEELING...

HAPPY SAD ANGRY TIRED ANNOYED SCARED

ANY SYMPTOMS?

CRAMPS SORE BREASTS HEAD ACHE BATHROOM TROUBLE NAUSEA ACNE

NOTES
_____
_____
_____

DATE:_____   PERIOD DAY # _____

FLOW: △ LIGHT   △△ MEDIUM   △△△ HEAVY

I'M FEELING...

HAPPY   SAD   ANGRY   TIRED   ANNOYED   SCARED

ANY SYMPTOMS?

CRAMPS   SORE BREASTS   HEAD ACHE   BATHROOM TROUBLE   NAUSEA   ACNE

NOTES
_____
_____
_____

DATE:_____   PERIOD DAY # _____

FLOW: △ LIGHT   △△ MEDIUM   △△△ HEAVY

I'M FEELING...

HAPPY   SAD   ANGRY   TIRED   ANNOYED   SCARED

ANY SYMPTOMS?

CRAMPS   SORE BREASTS   HEAD ACHE   BATHROOM TROUBLE   NAUSEA   ACNE

NOTES
_____
_____
_____

DATE:_____   PERIOD DAY #_____

FLOW: ◊ LIGHT   ◊◊ MEDIUM   ◊◊◊ HEAVY

I'M FEELING...

HAPPY   SAD   ANGRY   TIRED   ANNOYED   SCARED

ANY SYMPTOMS?

CRAMPS   SORE BREASTS   HEAD ACHE   BATHROOM TROUBLE   NAUSEA   ACNE

NOTES
_____
_____
_____

DATE:_____   PERIOD DAY #_____

FLOW: ◊ LIGHT   ◊◊ MEDIUM   ◊◊◊ HEAVY

I'M FEELING...

HAPPY   SAD   ANGRY   TIRED   ANNOYED   SCARED

ANY SYMPTOMS?

CRAMPS   SORE BREASTS   HEAD ACHE   BATHROOM TROUBLE   NAUSEA   ACNE

NOTES
_____
_____
_____

DATE:_____ PERIOD DAY #_____

FLOW: ◊ LIGHT ◊◊ MEDIUM ◊◊◊ HEAVY

I'M FEELING...

😊 HAPPY 😢 SAD 😠 ANGRY 😴 TIRED 😤 ANNOYED 😧 SCARED

ANY SYMPTOMS?

CRAMPS SORE BREASTS HEAD ACHE BATHROOM TROUBLE NAUSEA ACNE

NOTES
_____
_____
_____

DATE:_____ PERIOD DAY #_____

FLOW: ◊ LIGHT ◊◊ MEDIUM ◊◊◊ HEAVY

I'M FEELING...

😊 HAPPY 😢 SAD 😠 ANGRY 😴 TIRED 😤 ANNOYED 😧 SCARED

ANY SYMPTOMS?

CRAMPS SORE BREASTS HEAD ACHE BATHROOM TROUBLE NAUSEA ACNE

NOTES
_____
_____
_____

DATE:_____ PERIOD DAY #_____

FLOW: ◊ LIGHT   ◊◊ MEDIUM   ◊◊◊ HEAVY

I'M FEELING...

HAPPY   SAD   ANGRY   TIRED   ANNOYED   SCARED

ANY SYMPTOMS?

CRAMPS   SORE BREASTS   HEAD ACHE   BATHROOM TROUBLE   NAUSEA   ACNE

NOTES
_____
_____
_____

DATE:_____ PERIOD DAY #_____

FLOW: ◊ LIGHT   ◊◊ MEDIUM   ◊◊◊ HEAVY

I'M FEELING...

HAPPY   SAD   ANGRY   TIRED   ANNOYED   SCARED

ANY SYMPTOMS?

CRAMPS   SORE BREASTS   HEAD ACHE   BATHROOM TROUBLE   NAUSEA   ACNE

NOTES
_____
_____
_____

DATE:_____ PERIOD DAY #_____

FLOW: ◊ LIGHT   ◊◊ MEDIUM   ◊◊◊ HEAVY

I'M FEELING...

HAPPY   SAD   ANGRY   TIRED   ANNOYED   SCARED

ANY SYMPTOMS?

CRAMPS   SORE BREASTS   HEAD ACHE   BATHROOM TROUBLE   NAUSEA   ACNE

NOTES
_____
_____
_____

DATE:_____ PERIOD DAY #_____

FLOW: ◊ LIGHT   ◊◊ MEDIUM   ◊◊◊ HEAVY

I'M FEELING...

HAPPY   SAD   ANGRY   TIRED   ANNOYED   SCARED

ANY SYMPTOMS?

CRAMPS   SORE BREASTS   HEAD ACHE   BATHROOM TROUBLE   NAUSEA   ACNE

NOTES
_____
_____
_____

DATE:_____ PERIOD DAY # _____

FLOW: 🌢 LIGHT 🌢🌢 MEDIUM 🌢🌢🌢 HEAVY

I'M FEELING...

HAPPY SAD ANGRY TIRED ANNOYED SCARED

ANY SYMPTOMS?

CRAMPS SORE BREASTS HEAD ACHE BATHROOM TROUBLE NAUSEA ACNE

NOTES
_____
_____
_____

DATE:_____ PERIOD DAY # _____

FLOW: 🌢 LIGHT 🌢🌢 MEDIUM 🌢🌢🌢 HEAVY

I'M FEELING...

HAPPY SAD ANGRY TIRED ANNOYED SCARED

ANY SYMPTOMS?

CRAMPS SORE BREASTS HEAD ACHE BATHROOM TROUBLE NAUSEA ACNE

NOTES
_____
_____
_____

DATE:_____ PERIOD DAY # _____

FLOW: △ LIGHT △△ MEDIUM △△△ HEAVY

I'M FEELING...

😊 HAPPY 🏠 SAD 😠 ANGRY 😴 TIRED 😤 ANNOYED 😨 SCARED

ANY SYMPTOMS?

CRAMPS SORE BREASTS HEAD ACHE BATHROOM TROUBLE NAUSEA ACNE

NOTES _____
_____
_____

DATE:_____ PERIOD DAY # _____

FLOW: △ LIGHT △△ MEDIUM △△△ HEAVY

I'M FEELING...

😊 HAPPY 🏠 SAD 😠 ANGRY 😴 TIRED 😤 ANNOYED 😨 SCARED

ANY SYMPTOMS?

CRAMPS SORE BREASTS HEAD ACHE BATHROOM TROUBLE NAUSEA ACNE

NOTES _____
_____
_____

DATE:_____ PERIOD DAY #_____

FLOW: 🌢 LIGHT   🌢🌢 MEDIUM   🌢🌢🌢 HEAVY

I'M FEELING...

HAPPY   SAD   ANGRY   TIRED   ANNOYED   SCARED

ANY SYMPTOMS?

CRAMPS   SORE BREASTS   HEAD ACHE   BATHROOM TROUBLE   NAUSEA   ACNE

NOTES
_____
_____
_____

DATE:_____ PERIOD DAY #_____

FLOW: 🌢 LIGHT   🌢🌢 MEDIUM   🌢🌢🌢 HEAVY

I'M FEELING...

HAPPY   SAD   ANGRY   TIRED   ANNOYED   SCARED

ANY SYMPTOMS?

CRAMPS   SORE BREASTS   HEAD ACHE   BATHROOM TROUBLE   NAUSEA   ACNE

NOTES
_____
_____
_____

DATE:_____ PERIOD DAY #_____

FLOW: 🌢 LIGHT   🌢🌢 MEDIUM   🌢🌢🌢 HEAVY

I'M FEELING...

HAPPY   SAD   ANGRY   TIRED   ANNOYED   SCARED

ANY SYMPTOMS?

CRAMPS   SORE BREASTS   HEAD ACHE   BATHROOM TROUBLE   NAUSEA   ACNE

NOTES
_____
_____
_____

DATE:_____ PERIOD DAY #_____

FLOW: 🌢 LIGHT   🌢🌢 MEDIUM   🌢🌢🌢 HEAVY

I'M FEELING...

HAPPY   SAD   ANGRY   TIRED   ANNOYED   SCARED

ANY SYMPTOMS?

CRAMPS   SORE BREASTS   HEAD ACHE   BATHROOM TROUBLE   NAUSEA   ACNE

NOTES
_____
_____
_____

DATE:_____ PERIOD DAY #_____

FLOW: ◊ LIGHT   ◊◊ MEDIUM   ◊◊◊ HEAVY

I'M FEELING...

HAPPY   SAD   ANGRY   TIRED   ANNOYED   SCARED

ANY SYMPTOMS?

CRAMPS   SORE BREASTS   HEAD ACHE   BATHROOM TROUBLE   NAUSEA   ACNE

NOTES
_____
_____
_____

DATE:_____ PERIOD DAY #_____

FLOW: ◊ LIGHT   ◊◊ MEDIUM   ◊◊◊ HEAVY

I'M FEELING...

HAPPY   SAD   ANGRY   TIRED   ANNOYED   SCARED

ANY SYMPTOMS?

CRAMPS   SORE BREASTS   HEAD ACHE   BATHROOM TROUBLE   NAUSEA   ACNE

NOTES
_____
_____
_____

DATE:_____ PERIOD DAY #_____

FLOW: 🌢 LIGHT   🌢🌢 MEDIUM   🌢🌢🌢 HEAVY

I'M FEELING...

HAPPY   SAD   ANGRY   TIRED   ANNOYED   SCARED

ANY SYMPTOMS?

CRAMPS   SORE BREASTS   HEAD ACHE   BATHROOM TROUBLE   NAUSEA   ACNE

NOTES
_____
_____
_____

DATE:_____ PERIOD DAY #_____

FLOW: 🌢 LIGHT   🌢🌢 MEDIUM   🌢🌢🌢 HEAVY

I'M FEELING...

HAPPY   SAD   ANGRY   TIRED   ANNOYED   SCARED

ANY SYMPTOMS?

CRAMPS   SORE BREASTS   HEAD ACHE   BATHROOM TROUBLE   NAUSEA   ACNE

NOTES
_____
_____
_____

DATE:_____ PERIOD DAY #_____

FLOW: 🜄 LIGHT 🜄🜄 MEDIUM 🜄🜄🜄 HEAVY

I'M FEELING...

😊 HAPPY 😢 SAD 😠 ANGRY 😴 TIRED 😤 ANNOYED 😟 SCARED

ANY SYMPTOMS?

CRAMPS SORE BREASTS HEAD ACHE BATHROOM TROUBLE NAUSEA ACNE

NOTES
_____
_____
_____

DATE:_____ PERIOD DAY #_____

FLOW: 🜄 LIGHT 🜄🜄 MEDIUM 🜄🜄🜄 HEAVY

I'M FEELING...

😊 HAPPY 😢 SAD 😠 ANGRY 😴 TIRED 😤 ANNOYED 😟 SCARED

ANY SYMPTOMS?

CRAMPS SORE BREASTS HEAD ACHE BATHROOM TROUBLE NAUSEA ACNE

NOTES
_____
_____
_____

DATE:_____   PERIOD DAY #_____

FLOW: ○ LIGHT   ○○ MEDIUM   ○○○ HEAVY

I'M FEELING...

HAPPY   SAD   ANGRY   TIRED   ANNOYED   SCARED

ANY SYMPTOMS?

CRAMPS   SORE BREASTS   HEAD ACHE   BATHROOM TROUBLE   NAUSEA   ACNE

NOTES
_____
_____
_____

DATE:_____   PERIOD DAY #_____

FLOW: ○ LIGHT   ○○ MEDIUM   ○○○ HEAVY

I'M FEELING...

HAPPY   SAD   ANGRY   TIRED   ANNOYED   SCARED

ANY SYMPTOMS?

CRAMPS   SORE BREASTS   HEAD ACHE   BATHROOM TROUBLE   NAUSEA   ACNE

NOTES
_____
_____
_____

DATE:_____ PERIOD DAY #_____

FLOW: 🜄 LIGHT 🜄🜄 MEDIUM 🜄🜄🜄 HEAVY

I'M FEELING...

HAPPY   SAD   ANGRY   TIRED   ANNOYED   SCARED

ANY SYMPTOMS?

CRAMPS   SORE BREASTS   HEAD ACHE   BATHROOM TROUBLE   NAUSEA   ACNE

NOTES
_____
_____
_____

DATE:_____ PERIOD DAY #_____

FLOW: 🜄 LIGHT 🜄🜄 MEDIUM 🜄🜄🜄 HEAVY

I'M FEELING...

HAPPY   SAD   ANGRY   TIRED   ANNOYED   SCARED

ANY SYMPTOMS?

CRAMPS   SORE BREASTS   HEAD ACHE   BATHROOM TROUBLE   NAUSEA   ACNE

NOTES
_____
_____
_____

DATE:_____ PERIOD DAY #_____

FLOW: △ LIGHT   △△ MEDIUM   △△△ HEAVY

I'M FEELING...

HAPPY   SAD   ANGRY   TIRED   ANNOYED   SCARED

ANY SYMPTOMS?

CRAMPS   SORE BREASTS   HEAD ACHE   BATHROOM TROUBLE   NAUSEA   ACNE

NOTES _____
_____
_____

DATE:_____ PERIOD DAY #_____

FLOW: △ LIGHT   △△ MEDIUM   △△△ HEAVY

I'M FEELING...

HAPPY   SAD   ANGRY   TIRED   ANNOYED   SCARED

ANY SYMPTOMS?

CRAMPS   SORE BREASTS   HEAD ACHE   BATHROOM TROUBLE   NAUSEA   ACNE

NOTES _____
_____
_____

DATE:_____ PERIOD DAY #_____

FLOW: △ LIGHT   △△ MEDIUM   △△△ HEAVY

I'M FEELING...

😊 HAPPY   😢 SAD   😠 ANGRY   😴 TIRED   😣 ANNOYED   😟 SCARED

ANY SYMPTOMS?

CRAMPS   SORE BREASTS   HEAD ACHE   BATHROOM TROUBLE   NAUSEA   ACNE

NOTES _____
_____
_____

DATE:_____ PERIOD DAY #_____

FLOW: △ LIGHT   △△ MEDIUM   △△△ HEAVY

I'M FEELING...

😊 HAPPY   😢 SAD   😠 ANGRY   😴 TIRED   😣 ANNOYED   😟 SCARED

ANY SYMPTOMS?

CRAMPS   SORE BREASTS   HEAD ACHE   BATHROOM TROUBLE   NAUSEA   ACNE

NOTES _____
_____
_____

DATE:_____ PERIOD DAY #_____

FLOW: ⬦ LIGHT   ⬦⬦ MEDIUM   ⬦⬦⬦ HEAVY

I'M FEELING...

😊 HAPPY   😢 SAD   😠 ANGRY   😴 TIRED   😤 ANNOYED   😧 SCARED

ANY SYMPTOMS?

CRAMPS   SORE BREASTS   HEAD ACHE   BATHROOM TROUBLE   NAUSEA   ACNE

NOTES
_____
_____
_____

DATE:_____ PERIOD DAY #_____

FLOW: ⬦ LIGHT   ⬦⬦ MEDIUM   ⬦⬦⬦ HEAVY

I'M FEELING...

😊 HAPPY   😢 SAD   😠 ANGRY   😴 TIRED   😤 ANNOYED   😧 SCARED

ANY SYMPTOMS?

CRAMPS   SORE BREASTS   HEAD ACHE   BATHROOM TROUBLE   NAUSEA   ACNE

NOTES
_____
_____
_____

DATE:_____ PERIOD DAY #_____

FLOW: △ LIGHT   △△ MEDIUM   △△△ HEAVY

I'M FEELING...

HAPPY   SAD   ANGRY   TIRED   ANNOYED   SCARED

ANY SYMPTOMS?

CRAMPS   SORE BREASTS   HEAD ACHE   BATHROOM TROUBLE   NAUSEA   ACNE

NOTES
_____
_____
_____

DATE:_____ PERIOD DAY #_____

FLOW: △ LIGHT   △△ MEDIUM   △△△ HEAVY

I'M FEELING...

HAPPY   SAD   ANGRY   TIRED   ANNOYED   SCARED

ANY SYMPTOMS?

CRAMPS   SORE BREASTS   HEAD ACHE   BATHROOM TROUBLE   NAUSEA   ACNE

NOTES
_____
_____
_____

DATE:_____ PERIOD DAY #_____

FLOW: ◊ LIGHT ◊◊ MEDIUM ◊◊◊ HEAVY

I'M FEELING...

😊 HAPPY 😢 SAD 😠 ANGRY 😴 TIRED 😤 ANNOYED 😧 SCARED

ANY SYMPTOMS?

CRAMPS SORE BREASTS HEAD ACHE BATHROOM TROUBLE NAUSEA ACNE

NOTES
_____
_____
_____

DATE:_____ PERIOD DAY #_____

FLOW: ◊ LIGHT ◊◊ MEDIUM ◊◊◊ HEAVY

I'M FEELING...

😊 HAPPY 😢 SAD 😠 ANGRY 😴 TIRED 😤 ANNOYED 😧 SCARED

ANY SYMPTOMS?

CRAMPS SORE BREASTS HEAD ACHE BATHROOM TROUBLE NAUSEA ACNE

NOTES
_____
_____
_____

DATE:_____ PERIOD DAY #_____

FLOW: 🌢 LIGHT 🌢🌢 MEDIUM 🌢🌢🌢 HEAVY

I'M FEELING...

HAPPY   SAD   ANGRY   TIRED   ANNOYED   SCARED

ANY SYMPTOMS?

CRAMPS   SORE BREASTS   HEAD ACHE   BATHROOM TROUBLE   NAUSEA   ACNE

NOTES _____
_____
_____

DATE:_____ PERIOD DAY #_____

FLOW: 🌢 LIGHT 🌢🌢 MEDIUM 🌢🌢🌢 HEAVY

I'M FEELING...

HAPPY   SAD   ANGRY   TIRED   ANNOYED   SCARED

ANY SYMPTOMS?

CRAMPS   SORE BREASTS   HEAD ACHE   BATHROOM TROUBLE   NAUSEA   ACNE

NOTES _____
_____
_____

DATE:_____ PERIOD DAY #_____

FLOW: 🜄 LIGHT 🜄🜄 MEDIUM 🜄🜄🜄 HEAVY

I'M FEELING...

😊 HAPPY 😢 SAD 😠 ANGRY 😴 TIRED 😤 ANNOYED 😨 SCARED

ANY SYMPTOMS?

CRAMPS SORE BREASTS HEAD ACHE BATHROOM TROUBLE NAUSEA ACNE

NOTES
_____
_____
_____

DATE:_____ PERIOD DAY #_____

FLOW: 🜄 LIGHT 🜄🜄 MEDIUM 🜄🜄🜄 HEAVY

I'M FEELING...

😊 HAPPY 😢 SAD 😠 ANGRY 😴 TIRED 😤 ANNOYED 😨 SCARED

ANY SYMPTOMS?

CRAMPS SORE BREASTS HEAD ACHE BATHROOM TROUBLE NAUSEA ACNE

NOTES
_____
_____
_____

DATE:_____   PERIOD DAY #_____

FLOW: ◊ LIGHT   ◊◊ MEDIUM   ◊◊◊ HEAVY

I'M FEELING...

HAPPY   SAD   ANGRY   TIRED   ANNOYED   SCARED

ANY SYMPTOMS?

CRAMPS   SORE BREASTS   HEAD ACHE   BATHROOM TROUBLE   NAUSEA   ACNE

NOTES
_____
_____
_____

DATE:_____   PERIOD DAY #_____

FLOW: ◊ LIGHT   ◊◊ MEDIUM   ◊◊◊ HEAVY

I'M FEELING...

HAPPY   SAD   ANGRY   TIRED   ANNOYED   SCARED

ANY SYMPTOMS?

CRAMPS   SORE BREASTS   HEAD ACHE   BATHROOM TROUBLE   NAUSEA   ACNE

NOTES
_____
_____
_____

DATE:_____   PERIOD DAY #_____

FLOW: ⬤ LIGHT   ⬤⬤ MEDIUM   ⬤⬤⬤ HEAVY

I'M FEELING...

😊 HAPPY   🙁 SAD   😣 ANGRY   😴 TIRED   😤 ANNOYED   😧 SCARED

ANY SYMPTOMS?

CRAMPS   SORE BREASTS   HEAD ACHE   BATHROOM TROUBLE   NAUSEA   ACNE

NOTES
_____
_____
_____

DATE:_____   PERIOD DAY #_____

FLOW: ⬤ LIGHT   ⬤⬤ MEDIUM   ⬤⬤⬤ HEAVY

I'M FEELING...

😊 HAPPY   🙁 SAD   😣 ANGRY   😴 TIRED   😤 ANNOYED   😧 SCARED

ANY SYMPTOMS?

CRAMPS   SORE BREASTS   HEAD ACHE   BATHROOM TROUBLE   NAUSEA   ACNE

NOTES
_____
_____
_____

DATE:_____ PERIOD DAY #_____

FLOW: ◊ LIGHT   ◊◊ MEDIUM   ◊◊◊ HEAVY

I'M FEELING...

HAPPY   SAD   ANGRY   TIRED   ANNOYED   SCARED

ANY SYMPTOMS?

CRAMPS   SORE BREASTS   HEAD ACHE   BATHROOM TROUBLE   NAUSEA   ACNE

NOTES
_____
_____
_____

DATE:_____ PERIOD DAY #_____

FLOW: ◊ LIGHT   ◊◊ MEDIUM   ◊◊◊ HEAVY

I'M FEELING...

HAPPY   SAD   ANGRY   TIRED   ANNOYED   SCARED

ANY SYMPTOMS?

CRAMPS   SORE BREASTS   HEAD ACHE   BATHROOM TROUBLE   NAUSEA   ACNE

NOTES
_____
_____
_____

DATE: _____ PERIOD DAY # _____

FLOW: ◊ LIGHT ◊◊ MEDIUM ◊◊◊ HEAVY

I'M FEELING...

HAPPY SAD ANGRY TIRED ANNOYED SCARED

ANY SYMPTOMS?

CRAMPS SORE BREASTS HEAD ACHE BATHROOM TROUBLE NAUSEA ACNE

NOTES
_____
_____
_____

DATE: _____ PERIOD DAY # _____

FLOW: ◊ LIGHT ◊◊ MEDIUM ◊◊◊ HEAVY

I'M FEELING...

HAPPY SAD ANGRY TIRED ANNOYED SCARED

ANY SYMPTOMS?

CRAMPS SORE BREASTS HEAD ACHE BATHROOM TROUBLE NAUSEA ACNE

NOTES
_____
_____
_____

DATE:_____   PERIOD DAY #_____

FLOW: ◊ LIGHT   ◊◊ MEDIUM   ◊◊◊ HEAVY

I'M FEELING...

😊 HAPPY   😢 SAD   😠 ANGRY   😴 TIRED   😤 ANNOYED   😦 SCARED

ANY SYMPTOMS?

CRAMPS   SORE BREASTS   HEAD ACHE   BATHROOM TROUBLE   NAUSEA   ACNE

NOTES
_____
_____
_____

DATE:_____   PERIOD DAY #_____

FLOW: ◊ LIGHT   ◊◊ MEDIUM   ◊◊◊ HEAVY

I'M FEELING...

😊 HAPPY   😢 SAD   😠 ANGRY   😴 TIRED   😤 ANNOYED   😦 SCARED

ANY SYMPTOMS?

CRAMPS   SORE BREASTS   HEAD ACHE   BATHROOM TROUBLE   NAUSEA   ACNE

NOTES
_____
_____
_____

DATE:_____ PERIOD DAY #_____

FLOW: 🌢 LIGHT 🌢🌢 MEDIUM 🌢🌢🌢 HEAVY

I'M FEELING...

😊 HAPPY   😢 SAD   😠 ANGRY   😴 TIRED   😒 ANNOYED   😧 SCARED

ANY SYMPTOMS?

CRAMPS   SORE BREASTS   HEAD ACHE   BATHROOM TROUBLE   NAUSEA   ACNE

NOTES _____
_____
_____

DATE:_____ PERIOD DAY #_____

FLOW: 🌢 LIGHT 🌢🌢 MEDIUM 🌢🌢🌢 HEAVY

I'M FEELING...

😊 HAPPY   😢 SAD   😠 ANGRY   😴 TIRED   😒 ANNOYED   😧 SCARED

ANY SYMPTOMS?

CRAMPS   SORE BREASTS   HEAD ACHE   BATHROOM TROUBLE   NAUSEA   ACNE

NOTES _____
_____
_____

DATE:_____ PERIOD DAY #_____

FLOW: 🌢 LIGHT   🌢🌢 MEDIUM   🌢🌢🌢 HEAVY

I'M FEELING...

HAPPY   SAD   ANGRY   TIRED   ANNOYED   SCARED

ANY SYMPTOMS?

CRAMPS   SORE BREASTS   HEAD ACHE   BATHROOM TROUBLE   NAUSEA   ACNE

NOTES
_____
_____
_____

DATE:_____ PERIOD DAY #_____

FLOW: 🌢 LIGHT   🌢🌢 MEDIUM   🌢🌢🌢 HEAVY

I'M FEELING...

HAPPY   SAD   ANGRY   TIRED   ANNOYED   SCARED

ANY SYMPTOMS?

CRAMPS   SORE BREASTS   HEAD ACHE   BATHROOM TROUBLE   NAUSEA   ACNE

NOTES
_____
_____
_____

DATE:_____ PERIOD DAY #_____

FLOW: ◊ LIGHT   ◊◊ MEDIUM   ◊◊◊ HEAVY

I'M FEELING...

HAPPY   SAD   ANGRY   TIRED   ANNOYED   SCARED

ANY SYMPTOMS?

CRAMPS   SORE BREASTS   HEAD ACHE   BATHROOM TROUBLE   NAUSEA   ACNE

NOTES
_____
_____
_____

DATE:_____ PERIOD DAY #_____

FLOW: ◊ LIGHT   ◊◊ MEDIUM   ◊◊◊ HEAVY

I'M FEELING...

HAPPY   SAD   ANGRY   TIRED   ANNOYED   SCARED

ANY SYMPTOMS?

CRAMPS   SORE BREASTS   HEAD ACHE   BATHROOM TROUBLE   NAUSEA   ACNE

NOTES
_____
_____
_____

DATE:_____ PERIOD DAY #_____

FLOW: ◊ LIGHT ◊◊ MEDIUM ◊◊◊ HEAVY

I'M FEELING...

HAPPY　　SAD　　ANGRY　　TIRED　　ANNOYED　　SCARED

ANY SYMPTOMS?

CRAMPS　SORE BREASTS　HEAD ACHE　BATHROOM TROUBLE　NAUSEA　ACNE

NOTES
_____
_____
_____

DATE:_____ PERIOD DAY #_____

FLOW: ◊ LIGHT ◊◊ MEDIUM ◊◊◊ HEAVY

I'M FEELING...

HAPPY　　SAD　　ANGRY　　TIRED　　ANNOYED　　SCARED

ANY SYMPTOMS?

CRAMPS　SORE BREASTS　HEAD ACHE　BATHROOM TROUBLE　NAUSEA　ACNE

NOTES
_____
_____
_____

DATE:_____ PERIOD DAY #_____

FLOW: ◊ LIGHT   ◊◊ MEDIUM   ◊◊◊ HEAVY

I'M FEELING...

HAPPY SAD ANGRY TIRED ANNOYED SCARED

ANY SYMPTOMS?

CRAMPS SORE BREASTS HEAD ACHE BATHROOM TROUBLE NAUSEA ACNE

NOTES _____
_____
_____

DATE:_____ PERIOD DAY #_____

FLOW: ◊ LIGHT   ◊◊ MEDIUM   ◊◊◊ HEAVY

I'M FEELING...

HAPPY SAD ANGRY TIRED ANNOYED SCARED

ANY SYMPTOMS?

CRAMPS SORE BREASTS HEAD ACHE BATHROOM TROUBLE NAUSEA ACNE

NOTES _____
_____
_____

DATE:_____   PERIOD DAY #_____

FLOW: ◊ LIGHT   ◊◊ MEDIUM   ◊◊◊ HEAVY

I'M FEELING...

HAPPY   SAD   ANGRY   TIRED   ANNOYED   SCARED

ANY SYMPTOMS?

CRAMPS   SORE BREASTS   HEAD ACHE   BATHROOM TROUBLE   NAUSEA   ACNE

NOTES
_____
_____
_____

DATE:_____   PERIOD DAY #_____

FLOW: ◊ LIGHT   ◊◊ MEDIUM   ◊◊◊ HEAVY

I'M FEELING...

HAPPY   SAD   ANGRY   TIRED   ANNOYED   SCARED

ANY SYMPTOMS?

CRAMPS   SORE BREASTS   HEAD ACHE   BATHROOM TROUBLE   NAUSEA   ACNE

NOTES
_____
_____
_____

DATE:_____ PERIOD DAY #_____

FLOW: LIGHT MEDIUM HEAVY

I'M FEELING...

HAPPY   SAD   ANGRY   TIRED   ANNOYED   SCARED

ANY SYMPTOMS?

CRAMPS   SORE BREASTS   HEAD ACHE   BATHROOM TROUBLE   NAUSEA   ACNE

NOTES
_____
_____
_____

DATE:_____ PERIOD DAY #_____

FLOW: LIGHT MEDIUM HEAVY

I'M FEELING...

HAPPY   SAD   ANGRY   TIRED   ANNOYED   SCARED

ANY SYMPTOMS?

CRAMPS   SORE BREASTS   HEAD ACHE   BATHROOM TROUBLE   NAUSEA   ACNE

NOTES
_____
_____
_____

DATE:_____ PERIOD DAY #_____

FLOW: △ LIGHT   △△ MEDIUM   △△△ HEAVY

I'M FEELING...

HAPPY   SAD   ANGRY   TIRED   ANNOYED   SCARED

ANY SYMPTOMS?

CRAMPS   SORE BREASTS   HEAD ACHE   BATHROOM TROUBLE   NAUSEA   ACNE

NOTES _____
_____
_____

DATE:_____ PERIOD DAY #_____

FLOW: △ LIGHT   △△ MEDIUM   △△△ HEAVY

I'M FEELING...

HAPPY   SAD   ANGRY   TIRED   ANNOYED   SCARED

ANY SYMPTOMS?

CRAMPS   SORE BREASTS   HEAD ACHE   BATHROOM TROUBLE   NAUSEA   ACNE

NOTES _____
_____
_____

DATE:_____ PERIOD DAY #_____

FLOW: LIGHT 𝟂 MEDIUM 𝟂𝟂 HEAVY 𝟂𝟂𝟂

I'M FEELING...

HAPPY   SAD   ANGRY   TIRED   ANNOYED   SCARED

ANY SYMPTOMS?

CRAMPS   SORE BREASTS   HEAD ACHE   BATHROOM TROUBLE   NAUSEA   ACNE

NOTES
_____
_____
_____

DATE:_____ PERIOD DAY #_____

FLOW: LIGHT 𝟂 MEDIUM 𝟂𝟂 HEAVY 𝟂𝟂𝟂

I'M FEELING...

HAPPY   SAD   ANGRY   TIRED   ANNOYED   SCARED

ANY SYMPTOMS?

CRAMPS   SORE BREASTS   HEAD ACHE   BATHROOM TROUBLE   NAUSEA   ACNE

NOTES
_____
_____
_____

DATE:_____ PERIOD DAY # _____

FLOW: ◊ LIGHT   ◊◊ MEDIUM   ◊◊◊ HEAVY

I'M FEELING...

HAPPY   SAD   ANGRY   TIRED   ANNOYED   SCARED

ANY SYMPTOMS?

CRAMPS   SORE BREASTS   HEAD ACHE   BATHROOM TROUBLE   NAUSEA   ACNE

NOTES
_____
_____
_____

DATE:_____ PERIOD DAY # _____

FLOW: ◊ LIGHT   ◊◊ MEDIUM   ◊◊◊ HEAVY

I'M FEELING...

HAPPY   SAD   ANGRY   TIRED   ANNOYED   SCARED

ANY SYMPTOMS?

CRAMPS   SORE BREASTS   HEAD ACHE   BATHROOM TROUBLE   NAUSEA   ACNE

NOTES
_____
_____
_____

DATE:_____ PERIOD DAY #_____

FLOW: ◊ LIGHT ◊◊ MEDIUM ◊◊◊ HEAVY

I'M FEELING...

HAPPY SAD ANGRY TIRED ANNOYED SCARED

ANY SYMPTOMS?

CRAMPS SORE BREASTS HEAD ACHE BATHROOM TROUBLE NAUSEA ACNE

NOTES
_____
_____
_____

DATE:_____ PERIOD DAY #_____

FLOW: ◊ LIGHT ◊◊ MEDIUM ◊◊◊ HEAVY

I'M FEELING...

HAPPY SAD ANGRY TIRED ANNOYED SCARED

ANY SYMPTOMS?

CRAMPS SORE BREASTS HEAD ACHE BATHROOM TROUBLE NAUSEA ACNE

NOTES
_____
_____
_____

DATE:_____ PERIOD DAY #_____

FLOW: 𝟬 LIGHT 𝟬𝟬 MEDIUM 𝟬𝟬𝟬 HEAVY

I'M FEELING...

HAPPY SAD ANGRY TIRED ANNOYED SCARED

ANY SYMPTOMS?

CRAMPS SORE BREASTS HEAD ACHE BATHROOM TROUBLE NAUSEA ACNE

NOTES
_____
_____
_____

DATE:_____ PERIOD DAY #_____

FLOW: 𝟬 LIGHT 𝟬𝟬 MEDIUM 𝟬𝟬𝟬 HEAVY

I'M FEELING...

HAPPY SAD ANGRY TIRED ANNOYED SCARED

ANY SYMPTOMS?

CRAMPS SORE BREASTS HEAD ACHE BATHROOM TROUBLE NAUSEA ACNE

NOTES
_____
_____
_____

DATE:_____ PERIOD DAY #_____

FLOW: 🌢 LIGHT 🌢🌢 MEDIUM 🌢🌢🌢 HEAVY

I'M FEELING...

😊 HAPPY   😢 SAD   😠 ANGRY   😴 TIRED   😒 ANNOYED   😨 SCARED

ANY SYMPTOMS?

CRAMPS   SORE BREASTS   HEAD ACHE   BATHROOM TROUBLE   NAUSEA   ACNE

NOTES _____
_____
_____

DATE:_____ PERIOD DAY #_____

FLOW: 🌢 LIGHT 🌢🌢 MEDIUM 🌢🌢🌢 HEAVY

I'M FEELING...

😊 HAPPY   😢 SAD   😠 ANGRY   😴 TIRED   😒 ANNOYED   😨 SCARED

ANY SYMPTOMS?

CRAMPS   SORE BREASTS   HEAD ACHE   BATHROOM TROUBLE   NAUSEA   ACNE

NOTES _____
_____
_____

DATE:_____   PERIOD DAY #_____

FLOW: ◊ LIGHT   ◊◊ MEDIUM   ◊◊◊ HEAVY

I'M FEELING...

HAPPY   SAD   ANGRY   TIRED   ANNOYED   SCARED

ANY SYMPTOMS?

CRAMPS   SORE BREASTS   HEAD ACHE   BATHROOM TROUBLE   NAUSEA   ACNE

NOTES
_____
_____
_____

DATE:_____   PERIOD DAY #_____

FLOW: ◊ LIGHT   ◊◊ MEDIUM   ◊◊◊ HEAVY

I'M FEELING...

HAPPY   SAD   ANGRY   TIRED   ANNOYED   SCARED

ANY SYMPTOMS?

CRAMPS   SORE BREASTS   HEAD ACHE   BATHROOM TROUBLE   NAUSEA   ACNE

NOTES
_____
_____
_____

DATE:_____ PERIOD DAY #_____

FLOW: 🌢 LIGHT   🌢🌢 MEDIUM   🌢🌢🌢 HEAVY

I'M FEELING...

HAPPY   SAD   ANGRY   TIRED   ANNOYED   SCARED

ANY SYMPTOMS?

CRAMPS   SORE BREASTS   HEAD ACHE   BATHROOM TROUBLE   NAUSEA   ACNE

NOTES
_____
_____
_____

DATE:_____ PERIOD DAY #_____

FLOW: 🌢 LIGHT   🌢🌢 MEDIUM   🌢🌢🌢 HEAVY

I'M FEELING...

HAPPY   SAD   ANGRY   TIRED   ANNOYED   SCARED

ANY SYMPTOMS?

CRAMPS   SORE BREASTS   HEAD ACHE   BATHROOM TROUBLE   NAUSEA   ACNE

NOTES
_____
_____
_____

DATE: _____ PERIOD DAY # _____

FLOW: ◊ LIGHT   ◊◊ MEDIUM   ◊◊◊ HEAVY

I'M FEELING...

HAPPY   SAD   ANGRY   TIRED   ANNOYED   SCARED

ANY SYMPTOMS?

CRAMPS   SORE BREASTS   HEAD ACHE   BATHROOM TROUBLE   NAUSEA   ACNE

NOTES
_____
_____
_____

DATE: _____ PERIOD DAY # _____

FLOW: ◊ LIGHT   ◊◊ MEDIUM   ◊◊◊ HEAVY

I'M FEELING...

HAPPY   SAD   ANGRY   TIRED   ANNOYED   SCARED

ANY SYMPTOMS?

CRAMPS   SORE BREASTS   HEAD ACHE   BATHROOM TROUBLE   NAUSEA   ACNE

NOTES
_____
_____
_____

DATE:_____ PERIOD DAY #_____

FLOW: ⬦ LIGHT   ⬦⬦ MEDIUM   ⬦⬦⬦ HEAVY

I'M FEELING...

HAPPY   SAD   ANGRY   TIRED   ANNOYED   SCARED

ANY SYMPTOMS?

CRAMPS   SORE BREASTS   HEAD ACHE   BATHROOM TROUBLE   NAUSEA   ACNE

NOTES
_____
_____
_____

DATE:_____ PERIOD DAY #_____

FLOW: ⬦ LIGHT   ⬦⬦ MEDIUM   ⬦⬦⬦ HEAVY

I'M FEELING...

HAPPY   SAD   ANGRY   TIRED   ANNOYED   SCARED

ANY SYMPTOMS?

CRAMPS   SORE BREASTS   HEAD ACHE   BATHROOM TROUBLE   NAUSEA   ACNE

NOTES
_____
_____
_____

DATE:_____ PERIOD DAY #_____

FLOW: △ LIGHT △△ MEDIUM △△△ HEAVY

I'M FEELING...

HAPPY SAD ANGRY TIRED ANNOYED SCARED

ANY SYMPTOMS?

CRAMPS SORE BREASTS HEAD ACHE BATHROOM TROUBLE NAUSEA ACNE

NOTES _____
_____
_____

DATE:_____ PERIOD DAY #_____

FLOW: △ LIGHT △△ MEDIUM △△△ HEAVY

I'M FEELING...

HAPPY SAD ANGRY TIRED ANNOYED SCARED

ANY SYMPTOMS?

CRAMPS SORE BREASTS HEAD ACHE BATHROOM TROUBLE NAUSEA ACNE

NOTES _____
_____
_____

DATE:_____ PERIOD DAY #_____

FLOW: 🌢 LIGHT 🌢🌢 MEDIUM 🌢🌢🌢 HEAVY

I'M FEELING...

HAPPY   SAD   ANGRY   TIRED   ANNOYED   SCARED

ANY SYMPTOMS?

CRAMPS   SORE BREASTS   HEAD ACHE   BATHROOM TROUBLE   NAUSEA   ACNE

NOTES
_____
_____
_____

DATE:_____ PERIOD DAY #_____

FLOW: 🌢 LIGHT 🌢🌢 MEDIUM 🌢🌢🌢 HEAVY

I'M FEELING...

HAPPY   SAD   ANGRY   TIRED   ANNOYED   SCARED

ANY SYMPTOMS?

CRAMPS   SORE BREASTS   HEAD ACHE   BATHROOM TROUBLE   NAUSEA   ACNE

NOTES
_____
_____
_____

DATE:_____ PERIOD DAY # _____

FLOW: △ LIGHT △△ MEDIUM △△△ HEAVY

I'M FEELING...

😊 HAPPY 😢 SAD 😠 ANGRY 😴 TIRED 😤 ANNOYED 😧 SCARED

ANY SYMPTOMS?

CRAMPS SORE BREASTS HEAD ACHE BATHROOM TROUBLE NAUSEA ACNE

NOTES
_____
_____
_____

DATE:_____ PERIOD DAY # _____

FLOW: △ LIGHT △△ MEDIUM △△△ HEAVY

I'M FEELING...

😊 HAPPY 😢 SAD 😠 ANGRY 😴 TIRED 😤 ANNOYED 😧 SCARED

ANY SYMPTOMS?

CRAMPS SORE BREASTS HEAD ACHE BATHROOM TROUBLE NAUSEA ACNE

NOTES
_____
_____
_____

DATE:_____ PERIOD DAY #_____

FLOW: LIGHT   MEDIUM   HEAVY

I'M FEELING...

HAPPY   SAD   ANGRY   TIRED   ANNOYED   SCARED

ANY SYMPTOMS?

CRAMPS   SORE BREASTS   HEAD ACHE   BATHROOM TROUBLE   NAUSEA   ACNE

NOTES
_____
_____
_____

DATE:_____ PERIOD DAY #_____

FLOW: LIGHT   MEDIUM   HEAVY

I'M FEELING...

HAPPY   SAD   ANGRY   TIRED   ANNOYED   SCARED

ANY SYMPTOMS?

CRAMPS   SORE BREASTS   HEAD ACHE   BATHROOM TROUBLE   NAUSEA   ACNE

NOTES
_____
_____
_____

DATE:_____   PERIOD DAY #_____

FLOW: ◊ LIGHT   ◊◊ MEDIUM   ◊◊◊ HEAVY

I'M FEELING...

HAPPY   SAD   ANGRY   TIRED   ANNOYED   SCARED

ANY SYMPTOMS?

CRAMPS   SORE BREASTS   HEAD ACHE   BATHROOM TROUBLE   NAUSEA   ACNE

NOTES
_____
_____
_____

DATE:_____   PERIOD DAY #_____

FLOW: ◊ LIGHT   ◊◊ MEDIUM   ◊◊◊ HEAVY

I'M FEELING...

HAPPY   SAD   ANGRY   TIRED   ANNOYED   SCARED

ANY SYMPTOMS?

CRAMPS   SORE BREASTS   HEAD ACHE   BATHROOM TROUBLE   NAUSEA   ACNE

NOTES
_____
_____
_____

DATE: _____ PERIOD DAY # _____

FLOW: ◊ LIGHT ◊◊ MEDIUM ◊◊◊ HEAVY

I'M FEELING...

😊 HAPPY   😢 SAD   😠 ANGRY   😴 TIRED   😤 ANNOYED   😧 SCARED

ANY SYMPTOMS?

CRAMPS   SORE BREASTS   HEAD ACHE   BATHROOM TROUBLE   NAUSEA   ACNE

NOTES
_____
_____
_____

DATE: _____ PERIOD DAY # _____

FLOW: ◊ LIGHT ◊◊ MEDIUM ◊◊◊ HEAVY

I'M FEELING...

😊 HAPPY   😢 SAD   😠 ANGRY   😴 TIRED   😤 ANNOYED   😧 SCARED

ANY SYMPTOMS?

CRAMPS   SORE BREASTS   HEAD ACHE   BATHROOM TROUBLE   NAUSEA   ACNE

NOTES
_____
_____
_____

DATE:_____ PERIOD DAY #_____

FLOW: ⬦ LIGHT ⬦⬦ MEDIUM ⬦⬦⬦ HEAVY

I'M FEELING...

😊 HAPPY 😢 SAD 😠 ANGRY 😴 TIRED 😤 ANNOYED 😦 SCARED

ANY SYMPTOMS?

CRAMPS SORE BREASTS HEAD ACHE BATHROOM TROUBLE NAUSEA ACNE

NOTES
_____
_____
_____

DATE:_____ PERIOD DAY #_____

FLOW: ⬦ LIGHT ⬦⬦ MEDIUM ⬦⬦⬦ HEAVY

I'M FEELING...

😊 HAPPY 😢 SAD 😠 ANGRY 😴 TIRED 😤 ANNOYED 😦 SCARED

ANY SYMPTOMS?

CRAMPS SORE BREASTS HEAD ACHE BATHROOM TROUBLE NAUSEA ACNE

NOTES
_____
_____
_____

DATE:_____ PERIOD DAY #_____

FLOW: ◊ LIGHT   ◊◊ MEDIUM   ◊◊◊ HEAVY

I'M FEELING...

HAPPY   SAD   ANGRY   TIRED   ANNOYED   SCARED

ANY SYMPTOMS?

CRAMPS   SORE BREASTS   HEAD ACHE   BATHROOM TROUBLE   NAUSEA   ACNE

NOTES _____
_____
_____

DATE:_____ PERIOD DAY #_____

FLOW: ◊ LIGHT   ◊◊ MEDIUM   ◊◊◊ HEAVY

I'M FEELING...

HAPPY   SAD   ANGRY   TIRED   ANNOYED   SCARED

ANY SYMPTOMS?

CRAMPS   SORE BREASTS   HEAD ACHE   BATHROOM TROUBLE   NAUSEA   ACNE

NOTES _____
_____
_____

DATE:_____ PERIOD DAY #_____

FLOW: 🜄 LIGHT   🜄🜄 MEDIUM   🜄🜄🜄 HEAVY

I'M FEELING...

HAPPY   SAD   ANGRY   TIRED   ANNOYED   SCARED

ANY SYMPTOMS?

CRAMPS   SORE BREASTS   HEAD ACHE   BATHROOM TROUBLE   NAUSEA   ACNE

NOTES
_____
_____
_____

DATE:_____ PERIOD DAY #_____

FLOW: 🜄 LIGHT   🜄🜄 MEDIUM   🜄🜄🜄 HEAVY

I'M FEELING...

HAPPY   SAD   ANGRY   TIRED   ANNOYED   SCARED

ANY SYMPTOMS?

CRAMPS   SORE BREASTS   HEAD ACHE   BATHROOM TROUBLE   NAUSEA   ACNE

NOTES
_____
_____
_____

DATE:_____ PERIOD DAY # _____

FLOW: ⬦ LIGHT ⬦⬦ MEDIUM ⬦⬦⬦ HEAVY

I'M FEELING...

HAPPY SAD ANGRY TIRED ANNOYED SCARED

ANY SYMPTOMS?

CRAMPS SORE BREASTS HEAD ACHE BATHROOM TROUBLE NAUSEA ACNE

NOTES
_____
_____
_____

DATE:_____ PERIOD DAY # _____

FLOW: ⬦ LIGHT ⬦⬦ MEDIUM ⬦⬦⬦ HEAVY

I'M FEELING...

HAPPY SAD ANGRY TIRED ANNOYED SCARED

ANY SYMPTOMS?

CRAMPS SORE BREASTS HEAD ACHE BATHROOM TROUBLE NAUSEA ACNE

NOTES
_____
_____
_____

DATE:_____   PERIOD DAY # _____

FLOW: ◊ LIGHT   ◊◊ MEDIUM   ◊◊◊ HEAVY

I'M FEELING...

HAPPY   SAD   ANGRY   TIRED   ANNOYED   SCARED

ANY SYMPTOMS?

CRAMPS   SORE BREASTS   HEAD ACHE   BATHROOM TROUBLE   NAUSEA   ACNE

NOTES
_____
_____
_____

DATE:_____   PERIOD DAY # _____

FLOW: ◊ LIGHT   ◊◊ MEDIUM   ◊◊◊ HEAVY

I'M FEELING...

HAPPY   SAD   ANGRY   TIRED   ANNOYED   SCARED

ANY SYMPTOMS?

CRAMPS   SORE BREASTS   HEAD ACHE   BATHROOM TROUBLE   NAUSEA   ACNE

NOTES
_____
_____
_____

DATE:_____ PERIOD DAY #_____

FLOW: LIGHT MEDIUM HEAVY

I'M FEELING...

HAPPY SAD ANGRY TIRED ANNOYED SCARED

ANY SYMPTOMS?

CRAMPS SORE BREASTS HEAD ACHE BATHROOM TROUBLE NAUSEA ACNE

NOTES
_____
_____
_____

DATE:_____ PERIOD DAY #_____

FLOW: LIGHT MEDIUM HEAVY

I'M FEELING...

HAPPY SAD ANGRY TIRED ANNOYED SCARED

ANY SYMPTOMS?

CRAMPS SORE BREASTS HEAD ACHE BATHROOM TROUBLE NAUSEA ACNE

NOTES
_____
_____
_____

DATE:_____ PERIOD DAY # _____

FLOW: 🌢 LIGHT   🌢🌢 MEDIUM   🌢🌢🌢 HEAVY

I'M FEELING...

HAPPY   SAD   ANGRY   TIRED   ANNOYED   SCARED

ANY SYMPTOMS?

CRAMPS   SORE BREASTS   HEAD ACHE   BATHROOM TROUBLE   NAUSEA   ACNE

NOTES
_____
_____
_____

DATE:_____ PERIOD DAY # _____

FLOW: 🌢 LIGHT   🌢🌢 MEDIUM   🌢🌢🌢 HEAVY

I'M FEELING...

HAPPY   SAD   ANGRY   TIRED   ANNOYED   SCARED

ANY SYMPTOMS?

CRAMPS   SORE BREASTS   HEAD ACHE   BATHROOM TROUBLE   NAUSEA   ACNE

NOTES
_____
_____
_____

DATE:_____ PERIOD DAY #_____

FLOW: 🌢 LIGHT   🌢🌢 MEDIUM   🌢🌢🌢 HEAVY

I'M FEELING...

😊 HAPPY   😢 SAD   😠 ANGRY   😪 TIRED   😤 ANNOYED   😦 SCARED

ANY SYMPTOMS?

CRAMPS   SORE BREASTS   HEAD ACHE   BATHROOM TROUBLE   NAUSEA   ACNE

NOTES _____
_____
_____

DATE:_____ PERIOD DAY #_____

FLOW: 🌢 LIGHT   🌢🌢 MEDIUM   🌢🌢🌢 HEAVY

I'M FEELING...

😊 HAPPY   😢 SAD   😠 ANGRY   😪 TIRED   😤 ANNOYED   😦 SCARED

ANY SYMPTOMS?

CRAMPS   SORE BREASTS   HEAD ACHE   BATHROOM TROUBLE   NAUSEA   ACNE

NOTES _____
_____
_____

DATE:_____ PERIOD DAY # _____

FLOW: 🌢 LIGHT 🌢🌢 MEDIUM 🌢🌢🌢 HEAVY

I'M FEELING...

HAPPY   SAD   ANGRY   TIRED   ANNOYED   SCARED

ANY SYMPTOMS?

CRAMPS   SORE BREASTS   HEAD ACHE   BATHROOM TROUBLE   NAUSEA   ACNE

NOTES
_____
_____
_____

DATE:_____ PERIOD DAY # _____

FLOW: 🌢 LIGHT 🌢🌢 MEDIUM 🌢🌢🌢 HEAVY

I'M FEELING...

HAPPY   SAD   ANGRY   TIRED   ANNOYED   SCARED

ANY SYMPTOMS?

CRAMPS   SORE BREASTS   HEAD ACHE   BATHROOM TROUBLE   NAUSEA   ACNE

NOTES
_____
_____
_____

DATE:_____ PERIOD DAY #_____

FLOW: 🌢 LIGHT   🌢🌢 MEDIUM   🌢🌢🌢 HEAVY

I'M FEELING...

😊 HAPPY   😢 SAD   😠 ANGRY   😴 TIRED   😑 ANNOYED   😦 SCARED

ANY SYMPTOMS?

CRAMPS   SORE BREASTS   HEAD ACHE   BATHROOM TROUBLE   NAUSEA   ACNE

NOTES
_____
_____
_____

DATE:_____ PERIOD DAY #_____

FLOW: 🌢 LIGHT   🌢🌢 MEDIUM   🌢🌢🌢 HEAVY

I'M FEELING...

😊 HAPPY   😢 SAD   😠 ANGRY   😴 TIRED   😑 ANNOYED   😦 SCARED

ANY SYMPTOMS?

CRAMPS   SORE BREASTS   HEAD ACHE   BATHROOM TROUBLE   NAUSEA   ACNE

NOTES
_____
_____
_____

DATE:_____   PERIOD DAY #_____

FLOW: ⬤ LIGHT   ⬤⬤ MEDIUM   ⬤⬤⬤ HEAVY

I'M FEELING...

HAPPY   SAD   ANGRY   TIRED   ANNOYED   SCARED

ANY SYMPTOMS?

CRAMPS   SORE BREASTS   HEAD ACHE   BATHROOM TROUBLE   NAUSEA   ACNE

NOTES
_____
_____
_____

DATE:_____   PERIOD DAY #_____

FLOW: ⬤ LIGHT   ⬤⬤ MEDIUM   ⬤⬤⬤ HEAVY

I'M FEELING...

HAPPY   SAD   ANGRY   TIRED   ANNOYED   SCARED

ANY SYMPTOMS?

CRAMPS   SORE BREASTS   HEAD ACHE   BATHROOM TROUBLE   NAUSEA   ACNE

NOTES
_____
_____
_____

DATE:_____ PERIOD DAY # _____

FLOW: △ LIGHT   △△ MEDIUM   △△△ HEAVY

I'M FEELING...

😊 HAPPY   😢 SAD   😠 ANGRY   😴 TIRED   😤 ANNOYED   😧 SCARED

ANY SYMPTOMS?

CRAMPS   SORE BREASTS   HEAD ACHE   BATHROOM TROUBLE   NAUSEA   ACNE

NOTES
_____
_____
_____

DATE:_____ PERIOD DAY # _____

FLOW: △ LIGHT   △△ MEDIUM   △△△ HEAVY

I'M FEELING...

😊 HAPPY   😢 SAD   😠 ANGRY   😴 TIRED   😤 ANNOYED   😧 SCARED

ANY SYMPTOMS?

CRAMPS   SORE BREASTS   HEAD ACHE   BATHROOM TROUBLE   NAUSEA   ACNE

NOTES
_____
_____
_____

DATE:_____ PERIOD DAY #_____

FLOW: 💧 LIGHT   💧💧 MEDIUM   💧💧💧 HEAVY

I'M FEELING...

HAPPY   SAD   ANGRY   TIRED   ANNOYED   SCARED

ANY SYMPTOMS?

CRAMPS   SORE BREASTS   HEAD ACHE   BATHROOM TROUBLE   NAUSEA   ACNE

NOTES
_____
_____
_____

DATE:_____ PERIOD DAY #_____

FLOW: 💧 LIGHT   💧💧 MEDIUM   💧💧💧 HEAVY

I'M FEELING...

HAPPY   SAD   ANGRY   TIRED   ANNOYED   SCARED

ANY SYMPTOMS?

CRAMPS   SORE BREASTS   HEAD ACHE   BATHROOM TROUBLE   NAUSEA   ACNE

NOTES
_____
_____
_____

DATE:_____ PERIOD DAY #_____

FLOW: LIGHT MEDIUM HEAVY

I'M FEELING...

HAPPY   SAD   ANGRY   TIRED   ANNOYED   SCARED

ANY SYMPTOMS?

CRAMPS   SORE BREASTS   HEAD ACHE   BATHROOM TROUBLE   NAUSEA   ACNE

NOTES _____
_____
_____
_____

DATE:_____ PERIOD DAY #_____

FLOW: LIGHT MEDIUM HEAVY

I'M FEELING...

HAPPY   SAD   ANGRY   TIRED   ANNOYED   SCARED

ANY SYMPTOMS?

CRAMPS   SORE BREASTS   HEAD ACHE   BATHROOM TROUBLE   NAUSEA   ACNE

NOTES _____
_____
_____
_____

DATE:_____   PERIOD DAY #_____

FLOW: ◊ LIGHT   ◊◊ MEDIUM   ◊◊◊ HEAVY

I'M FEELING...

HAPPY   SAD   ANGRY   TIRED   ANNOYED   SCARED

ANY SYMPTOMS?

CRAMPS   SORE BREASTS   HEAD ACHE   BATHROOM TROUBLE   NAUSEA   ACNE

NOTES
_____
_____
_____

DATE:_____   PERIOD DAY #_____

FLOW: ◊ LIGHT   ◊◊ MEDIUM   ◊◊◊ HEAVY

I'M FEELING...

HAPPY   SAD   ANGRY   TIRED   ANNOYED   SCARED

ANY SYMPTOMS?

CRAMPS   SORE BREASTS   HEAD ACHE   BATHROOM TROUBLE   NAUSEA   ACNE

NOTES
_____
_____
_____

DATE:_____ PERIOD DAY #_____

FLOW: LIGHT   MEDIUM   HEAVY

I'M FEELING...

HAPPY   SAD   ANGRY   TIRED   ANNOYED   SCARED

ANY SYMPTOMS?

CRAMPS   SORE BREASTS   HEAD ACHE   BATHROOM TROUBLE   NAUSEA   ACNE

NOTES
_____
_____
_____

DATE:_____ PERIOD DAY #_____

FLOW: LIGHT   MEDIUM   HEAVY

I'M FEELING...

HAPPY   SAD   ANGRY   TIRED   ANNOYED   SCARED

ANY SYMPTOMS?

CRAMPS   SORE BREASTS   HEAD ACHE   BATHROOM TROUBLE   NAUSEA   ACNE

NOTES
_____
_____
_____

DATE:_____ PERIOD DAY #_____

FLOW: 🌢 LIGHT   🌢🌢 MEDIUM   🌢🌢🌢 HEAVY

I'M FEELING...

HAPPY   SAD   ANGRY   TIRED   ANNOYED   SCARED

ANY SYMPTOMS?

CRAMPS   SORE BREASTS   HEAD ACHE   BATHROOM TROUBLE   NAUSEA   ACNE

NOTES
_____
_____
_____

DATE:_____ PERIOD DAY #_____

FLOW: 🌢 LIGHT   🌢🌢 MEDIUM   🌢🌢🌢 HEAVY

I'M FEELING...

HAPPY   SAD   ANGRY   TIRED   ANNOYED   SCARED

ANY SYMPTOMS?

CRAMPS   SORE BREASTS   HEAD ACHE   BATHROOM TROUBLE   NAUSEA   ACNE

NOTES
_____
_____
_____

DATE:_____ PERIOD DAY #_____

FLOW: LIGHT   MEDIUM   HEAVY

I'M FEELING...

HAPPY   SAD   ANGRY   TIRED   ANNOYED   SCARED

ANY SYMPTOMS?

CRAMPS   SORE BREASTS   HEAD ACHE   BATHROOM TROUBLE   NAUSEA   ACNE

NOTES
_____
_____
_____

DATE:_____ PERIOD DAY #_____

FLOW: LIGHT   MEDIUM   HEAVY

I'M FEELING...

HAPPY   SAD   ANGRY   TIRED   ANNOYED   SCARED

ANY SYMPTOMS?

CRAMPS   SORE BREASTS   HEAD ACHE   BATHROOM TROUBLE   NAUSEA   ACNE

NOTES
_____
_____
_____

DATE:_____ PERIOD DAY #_____

FLOW: 🜄 LIGHT   🜄🜄 MEDIUM   🜄🜄🜄 HEAVY

I'M FEELING...

😊 HAPPY 😢 SAD 😠 ANGRY 😴 TIRED 😤 ANNOYED 😧 SCARED

ANY SYMPTOMS?

CRAMPS SORE BREASTS HEAD ACHE BATHROOM TROUBLE NAUSEA ACNE

NOTES
_____
_____
_____

DATE:_____ PERIOD DAY #_____

FLOW: 🜄 LIGHT   🜄🜄 MEDIUM   🜄🜄🜄 HEAVY

I'M FEELING...

😊 HAPPY 😢 SAD 😠 ANGRY 😴 TIRED 😤 ANNOYED 😧 SCARED

ANY SYMPTOMS?

CRAMPS SORE BREASTS HEAD ACHE BATHROOM TROUBLE NAUSEA ACNE

NOTES
_____
_____
_____

DATE:_____ PERIOD DAY #_____

FLOW: ⬦ LIGHT ⬦⬦ MEDIUM ⬦⬦⬦ HEAVY

I'M FEELING...

😊 HAPPY   😢 SAD   😠 ANGRY   😴 TIRED   😤 ANNOYED   😨 SCARED

ANY SYMPTOMS?

CRAMPS   SORE BREASTS   HEAD ACHE   BATHROOM TROUBLE   NAUSEA   ACNE

NOTES
_____
_____
_____

DATE:_____ PERIOD DAY #_____

FLOW: ⬦ LIGHT ⬦⬦ MEDIUM ⬦⬦⬦ HEAVY

I'M FEELING...

😊 HAPPY   😢 SAD   😠 ANGRY   😴 TIRED   😤 ANNOYED   😨 SCARED

ANY SYMPTOMS?

CRAMPS   SORE BREASTS   HEAD ACHE   BATHROOM TROUBLE   NAUSEA   ACNE

NOTES
_____
_____
_____

DATE:_____ PERIOD DAY #_____

FLOW: 🌢 LIGHT 🌢🌢 MEDIUM 🌢🌢🌢 HEAVY

I'M FEELING...

😊 HAPPY   😢 SAD   😠 ANGRY   😴 TIRED   😤 ANNOYED   😧 SCARED

ANY SYMPTOMS?

CRAMPS   SORE BREASTS   HEAD ACHE   BATHROOM TROUBLE   NAUSEA   ACNE

NOTES
_____
_____
_____

DATE:_____ PERIOD DAY #_____

FLOW: 🌢 LIGHT 🌢🌢 MEDIUM 🌢🌢🌢 HEAVY

I'M FEELING...

😊 HAPPY   😢 SAD   😠 ANGRY   😴 TIRED   😤 ANNOYED   😧 SCARED

ANY SYMPTOMS?

CRAMPS   SORE BREASTS   HEAD ACHE   BATHROOM TROUBLE   NAUSEA   ACNE

NOTES
_____
_____
_____

DATE:_____ PERIOD DAY #_____

FLOW: ○ LIGHT   ○○ MEDIUM   ○○○ HEAVY

I'M FEELING...

HAPPY   SAD   ANGRY   TIRED   ANNOYED   SCARED

ANY SYMPTOMS?

CRAMPS   SORE BREASTS   HEAD ACHE   BATHROOM TROUBLE   NAUSEA   ACNE

NOTES
_____
_____
_____

DATE:_____ PERIOD DAY #_____

FLOW: ○ LIGHT   ○○ MEDIUM   ○○○ HEAVY

I'M FEELING...

HAPPY   SAD   ANGRY   TIRED   ANNOYED   SCARED

ANY SYMPTOMS?

CRAMPS   SORE BREASTS   HEAD ACHE   BATHROOM TROUBLE   NAUSEA   ACNE

NOTES
_____
_____
_____

DATE:_____ PERIOD DAY #_____

FLOW: 🌢 LIGHT   🌢🌢 MEDIUM   🌢🌢🌢 HEAVY

I'M FEELING...

HAPPY   SAD   ANGRY   TIRED   ANNOYED   SCARED

ANY SYMPTOMS?

CRAMPS   SORE BREASTS   HEAD ACHE   BATHROOM TROUBLE   NAUSEA   ACNE

NOTES
_____
_____
_____

DATE:_____ PERIOD DAY #_____

FLOW: 🌢 LIGHT   🌢🌢 MEDIUM   🌢🌢🌢 HEAVY

I'M FEELING...

HAPPY   SAD   ANGRY   TIRED   ANNOYED   SCARED

ANY SYMPTOMS?

CRAMPS   SORE BREASTS   HEAD ACHE   BATHROOM TROUBLE   NAUSEA   ACNE

NOTES
_____
_____
_____

DATE:_____ PERIOD DAY #_____

FLOW: △ LIGHT   △△ MEDIUM   △△△ HEAVY

I'M FEELING...

☺ HAPPY   ☹ SAD   😠 ANGRY   😫 TIRED   😤 ANNOYED   😯 SCARED

ANY SYMPTOMS?

CRAMPS   SORE BREASTS   HEAD ACHE   BATHROOM TROUBLE   NAUSEA   ACNE

NOTES
_____
_____
_____

DATE:_____ PERIOD DAY #_____

FLOW: △ LIGHT   △△ MEDIUM   △△△ HEAVY

I'M FEELING...

☺ HAPPY   ☹ SAD   😠 ANGRY   😫 TIRED   😤 ANNOYED   😯 SCARED

ANY SYMPTOMS?

CRAMPS   SORE BREASTS   HEAD ACHE   BATHROOM TROUBLE   NAUSEA   ACNE

NOTES
_____
_____
_____

DATE:_____   PERIOD DAY #_____

FLOW: ◊ LIGHT   ◊◊ MEDIUM   ◊◊◊ HEAVY

I'M FEELING...

HAPPY   SAD   ANGRY   TIRED   ANNOYED   SCARED

ANY SYMPTOMS?

CRAMPS   SORE BREASTS   HEAD ACHE   BATHROOM TROUBLE   NAUSEA   ACNE

NOTES
_____
_____
_____

DATE:_____   PERIOD DAY #_____

FLOW: ◊ LIGHT   ◊◊ MEDIUM   ◊◊◊ HEAVY

I'M FEELING...

HAPPY   SAD   ANGRY   TIRED   ANNOYED   SCARED

ANY SYMPTOMS?

CRAMPS   SORE BREASTS   HEAD ACHE   BATHROOM TROUBLE   NAUSEA   ACNE

NOTES
_____
_____
_____

DATE:_____ PERIOD DAY #_____

FLOW: △ LIGHT   △△ MEDIUM   △△△ HEAVY

I'M FEELING...

HAPPY   SAD   ANGRY   TIRED   ANNOYED   SCARED

ANY SYMPTOMS?

CRAMPS   SORE BREASTS   HEAD ACHE   BATHROOM TROUBLE   NAUSEA   ACNE

NOTES
_____
_____
_____

DATE:_____ PERIOD DAY #_____

FLOW: △ LIGHT   △△ MEDIUM   △△△ HEAVY

I'M FEELING...

HAPPY   SAD   ANGRY   TIRED   ANNOYED   SCARED

ANY SYMPTOMS?

CRAMPS   SORE BREASTS   HEAD ACHE   BATHROOM TROUBLE   NAUSEA   ACNE

NOTES
_____
_____
_____

DATE:_____ PERIOD DAY #_____

FLOW: 🌢 LIGHT   🌢🌢 MEDIUM   🌢🌢🌢 HEAVY

I'M FEELING...

😊 HAPPY   😢 SAD   😠 ANGRY   😴 TIRED   😤 ANNOYED   😧 SCARED

ANY SYMPTOMS?

CRAMPS   SORE BREASTS   HEAD ACHE   BATHROOM TROUBLE   NAUSEA   ACNE

NOTES _____
_____
_____

DATE:_____ PERIOD DAY #_____

FLOW: 🌢 LIGHT   🌢🌢 MEDIUM   🌢🌢🌢 HEAVY

I'M FEELING...

😊 HAPPY   😢 SAD   😠 ANGRY   😴 TIRED   😤 ANNOYED   😧 SCARED

ANY SYMPTOMS?

CRAMPS   SORE BREASTS   HEAD ACHE   BATHROOM TROUBLE   NAUSEA   ACNE

NOTES _____
_____
_____

DATE:_____ PERIOD DAY #_____

FLOW: ◊ LIGHT   ◊◊ MEDIUM   ◊◊◊ HEAVY

I'M FEELING...

HAPPY   SAD   ANGRY   TIRED   ANNOYED   SCARED

ANY SYMPTOMS?

CRAMPS   SORE BREASTS   HEAD ACHE   BATHROOM TROUBLE   NAUSEA   ACNE

NOTES
_____
_____
_____

DATE:_____ PERIOD DAY #_____

FLOW: ◊ LIGHT   ◊◊ MEDIUM   ◊◊◊ HEAVY

I'M FEELING...

HAPPY   SAD   ANGRY   TIRED   ANNOYED   SCARED

ANY SYMPTOMS?

CRAMPS   SORE BREASTS   HEAD ACHE   BATHROOM TROUBLE   NAUSEA   ACNE

NOTES
_____
_____
_____

DATE:_____ PERIOD DAY #_____

FLOW: 🌢 LIGHT 🌢🌢 MEDIUM 🌢🌢🌢 HEAVY

I'M FEELING...

HAPPY   SAD   ANGRY   TIRED   ANNOYED   SCARED

ANY SYMPTOMS?

CRAMPS   SORE BREASTS   HEAD ACHE   BATHROOM TROUBLE   NAUSEA   ACNE

NOTES _____
_____
_____

DATE:_____ PERIOD DAY #_____

FLOW: 🌢 LIGHT 🌢🌢 MEDIUM 🌢🌢🌢 HEAVY

I'M FEELING...

HAPPY   SAD   ANGRY   TIRED   ANNOYED   SCARED

ANY SYMPTOMS?

CRAMPS   SORE BREASTS   HEAD ACHE   BATHROOM TROUBLE   NAUSEA   ACNE

NOTES _____
_____
_____

DATE:_____   PERIOD DAY #_____

FLOW: ⬤ LIGHT   ⬤⬤ MEDIUM   ⬤⬤⬤ HEAVY

I'M FEELING...

HAPPY   SAD   ANGRY   TIRED   ANNOYED   SCARED

ANY SYMPTOMS?

CRAMPS   SORE BREASTS   HEAD ACHE   BATHROOM TROUBLE   NAUSEA   ACNE

NOTES _____
_____
_____

DATE:_____   PERIOD DAY #_____

FLOW: ⬤ LIGHT   ⬤⬤ MEDIUM   ⬤⬤⬤ HEAVY

I'M FEELING...

HAPPY   SAD   ANGRY   TIRED   ANNOYED   SCARED

ANY SYMPTOMS?

CRAMPS   SORE BREASTS   HEAD ACHE   BATHROOM TROUBLE   NAUSEA   ACNE

NOTES _____
_____
_____

DATE:_____ PERIOD DAY #_____

FLOW: ◊ LIGHT   ◊◊ MEDIUM   ◊◊◊ HEAVY

I'M FEELING...

HAPPY   SAD   ANGRY   TIRED   ANNOYED   SCARED

ANY SYMPTOMS?

CRAMPS   SORE BREASTS   HEAD ACHE   BATHROOM TROUBLE   NAUSEA   ACNE

NOTES
_____
_____
_____

DATE:_____ PERIOD DAY #_____

FLOW: ◊ LIGHT   ◊◊ MEDIUM   ◊◊◊ HEAVY

I'M FEELING...

HAPPY   SAD   ANGRY   TIRED   ANNOYED   SCARED

ANY SYMPTOMS?

CRAMPS   SORE BREASTS   HEAD ACHE   BATHROOM TROUBLE   NAUSEA   ACNE

NOTES
_____
_____
_____

DATE:_____ PERIOD DAY #_____

FLOW: 🌢 LIGHT   🌢🌢 MEDIUM   🌢🌢🌢 HEAVY

I'M FEELING...

HAPPY   SAD   ANGRY   TIRED   ANNOYED   SCARED

ANY SYMPTOMS?

CRAMPS   SORE BREASTS   HEAD ACHE   BATHROOM TROUBLE   NAUSEA   ACNE

NOTES _____
_____
_____

DATE:_____ PERIOD DAY #_____

FLOW: 🌢 LIGHT   🌢🌢 MEDIUM   🌢🌢🌢 HEAVY

I'M FEELING...

HAPPY   SAD   ANGRY   TIRED   ANNOYED   SCARED

ANY SYMPTOMS?

CRAMPS   SORE BREASTS   HEAD ACHE   BATHROOM TROUBLE   NAUSEA   ACNE

NOTES _____
_____
_____

DATE:_____ PERIOD DAY #_____

FLOW: 🌢 LIGHT 🌢🌢 MEDIUM 🌢🌢🌢 HEAVY

I'M FEELING...

HAPPY SAD ANGRY TIRED ANNOYED SCARED

ANY SYMPTOMS?

CRAMPS SORE BREASTS HEAD ACHE BATHROOM TROUBLE NAUSEA ACNE

NOTES
_____
_____
_____

DATE:_____ PERIOD DAY #_____

FLOW: 🌢 LIGHT 🌢🌢 MEDIUM 🌢🌢🌢 HEAVY

I'M FEELING...

HAPPY SAD ANGRY TIRED ANNOYED SCARED

ANY SYMPTOMS?

CRAMPS SORE BREASTS HEAD ACHE BATHROOM TROUBLE NAUSEA ACNE

NOTES
_____
_____
_____

DATE:_____ PERIOD DAY #_____

FLOW: LIGHT 💧 MEDIUM 💧💧 HEAVY 💧💧💧

I'M FEELING...

HAPPY SAD ANGRY TIRED ANNOYED SCARED

ANY SYMPTOMS?

CRAMPS SORE BREASTS HEAD ACHE BATHROOM TROUBLE NAUSEA ACNE

NOTES _____
_____
_____
_____

DATE:_____ PERIOD DAY #_____

FLOW: LIGHT 💧 MEDIUM 💧💧 HEAVY 💧💧💧

I'M FEELING...

HAPPY SAD ANGRY TIRED ANNOYED SCARED

ANY SYMPTOMS?

CRAMPS SORE BREASTS HEAD ACHE BATHROOM TROUBLE NAUSEA ACNE

NOTES _____
_____
_____
_____

Printed in Great Britain
by Amazon

78351676R00059